For Entrepreneurs and To be Entrepreneurs

My

I0482934

APPLE

is

Branded

The Step by Step Guide to Build Your Rich and Successful Brand...*Faster!*

By Success Coach Nilesh

DEDICATION

To my father, Dr. Manikrao Waghchoude,
for his
deep love, care, and trust in me

CONGRATULATIONS

Creating your brand is an ongoing process. As brands reap massive rewards, it is worth putting your time, money and resources in building your brand.

Congratulations on starting a journey that I know will change your life as you commit to the brand building process and change the lives of the people those will be touched by your brand.

Thank you!

Yours Sincerely,
Success Coach Nilesh

www.SuccessCoachNilesh.com

CONTENTS

ACKNOWLEDGMENTS

As Rumi, a 13th century Persian poet, has said, "You are not living on earth, you are passing through earth."

For my journey on earth, I am blessed to meet certain people who have helped me shape my life.

I would first like to thank my wife Meenal for patiently listening to my dreams and ambitions and for supporting my numerous attempts to make this book a best experience for you, the reader.

I would also like to thank my sister, Neelima, my brother-in-law and friend Jeevan, my mother Sunita, and my brother Sanket for their love and care.

Next, a huge thanks to my friends, clients and all the people who have helped me bring this book to you.

Everyone matters.

ABOUT THE AUTHOR

Nilesh Waghchoude (also known as Success Coach Nilesh) is a best-selling Author, Branding Expert and the Creator of Accelerated Success Techniques™.

He has spoken at London Youth Conference, London Business School, Bradford School of Management, College of Engineering Pune- COEP, Lila Poonawala Foundation, Maharashtra Mandal London, Junior Chamber International, UK etc.

He has also travelled and spoken in many countries in the world including USA, UK, Singapore, Thailand, Switzerland, France, Italy etc.

He has coached and consulted CEOs, Directors, Managers, Students, and Entrepreneurs etc.

However he started from very bottom. Nilesh was born and brought up in India where English was not even his first language. After studying at village and taluka levels he came to Pune (One of the big cities in India) to study engineering. He was overwhelmed by the people and life in city because he had never experienced that before. He had lack of self-confidence but had lots of self-doubts and negative beliefs. He even failed in his first year engineering exam. However he kept going and graduated from engineering in first class with distinction.

Nilesh started his professional career as a Car Design Engineer. After working in India for a couple of years he went to USA to work for his companies' clients.

His professional career was great but he wanted to pursue his dream of completing his MBA. To achieve his dream he quit his job and went to United Kingdom for his Business studies.

After completing his MBA, he got a job offer to work for

one of the most prestigious luxury car companies in the UK and he started his job. He was very happy with his job, but this happiness did not last long. Something was going to happen which transformed his life forever.

Due to the economic recession, his company undertook the lay-offs route. As Nilesh was fairly new in his job; he was amongst the people who got laid off.

This was a massive setback for Nilesh. He had a huge education loan to pay back and there were no signs of the economy recovering. He applied for thousands of jobs but what he got was only rejections.

Nothing seemed to be working for him. Nilesh began to think: How did he get here? How can he come out of this mess, survive and be successful?

At that moment he made a decision to change his bad situation and work diligently to become successful in his career.

He then started working part time for a very low paying job at Arts Centre where his job was to check tickets at the door of the venue.

During this time Nilesh also started his own Business consulting company. He realized that it is not our circumstances but our decisions that shape our lives & our future.

In his free time he started reading self-development books and listening to audio programs. He even attended LIVE training sessions, seminars and workshops by world-class people such as Tony Robbins, Les Brown, Harv Eker, Richard Branson, Donald Trump, Robert Kiyosaki, Brain Tracy etc. and his life started to get back on track.

Nilesh's perseverance resulted in him starting to deliver successful coaching and training sessions that transformed many people's lives and businesses.

During the first year of the company he was the finalist for the two prestigious awards by Institute of Business Consulting UK.

(Best Newcomer to Consulting and Most Outstanding Achievement towards Continuous Professional Development)

Nilesh now conducts Trainings, Consulting and one to one Coaching sessions.

Nilesh teaches those Precise, Proven and Powerful Tools & Strategies which will help you make FASTER Progress in your Career, Business and Life.

Using the principles he now teaches, Nilesh has transformed his own life, career, finances, health, and relationships.

He now works with professionals from all over the world to provide them smart strategies to make faster progress in their lives & businesses.

These strategies are made up of several critical secrets absolutely necessary for rapid & sustainable personal, professional and business success.

So please don't even think of missing the information revealed in his book and sessions.

For further details on his sessions, trainings & workshops please visit:

www.SuccessCoachNilesh.com

So far Nilesh has helped his clients in following areas:

- Increasing their Income by 40-300% by his Efficient Money Management System (EMMS)
- Improving their Leadership, Communication, Public speaking and Management skills to achieve Maximum Influence and Results in shorter time
- Developing Powerful Action Plans to Become More Efficient and Productive
- Feeling Confident at Work place
- Growing Self Confidence and Achieving Maximum Results
- Getting freedom from Fears and stress
- Increasing their Savings by 20-50% by his Strategic Financial Planning (SFP)
- Achieving their Personal Goals and Becoming Successful Strategically & Quickly
- Developing Marketing & Sales Strategies which will work in real life to achieve Business Turnaround & Long Lasting Growth
- Mastering the Skill of Time Management and Strategic Task Management (STM)
- Becoming an Expert to make Faster Progress in their Career and Life
- Gaining Confidence & Power during Interviews.
- Designing Personal Blueprint for Long-term Success
- & Many More topics to suit his clients' Special Needs

For further details on his sessions, trainings & workshops please visit:

www.SuccessCoachNilesh.com

P.S. Success Coach Nilesh's 'Go For Success' - book is available on Amazon-worldwide. It gives the most real 6 steps to Success in your life, career and business. It will save your time and money by providing you the real 6 steps to your Success.

There is always space at the Top and when you are at the Top, there is always market for you. Always Aim High!

~ Success Coach Nilesh

My Apple is Branded

Introduction

Thank you for picking up this book! There may be any number of reasons you are reading this book. But if you are looking for some proven and powerful strategies to help you in creating your personal or business brand (and that too Faster), then this is the right book for you.

I am sure you will agree with me when I say that between time and money, time is most valuable. Because, you can get the lost money back but you cannot get the lost time back.

Also, we have a definite lifespan, which means we have limited time on this earth. Hence, it makes perfect sense to become successful as soon as we can and start living our dream life as long as we can.

My aim is to share with you those secrets which will help you become a successful and outstanding brand, strategically, systematically, and quickly.

Maybe you have a business idea or you own a business, or you have a dream of having a successful career or retiring early from your professional life to go on a world tour or simply to get out of debt and live free. Whatever the case may be, this book is all about revealing the system used by successful people and businesses around the world. None of these strategies are made up, but they have been carefully studied, tried, and tested. They are proven and powerful, and they work in the real world.

Before we proceed I want to know, is your dream of creating an Outstanding Brand worth achieving? If YES, then do yourself a favor and make it one of the necessities in your life. As you read this book, get a pen and paper, mute your phone, and ignore Facebook for a little while. They will still be there when you are done!

As your dreams are truly worth achieving, they are truly worth giving your full attention for the short time it will take you to follow along with me. I am sure that as you read this book, you will start picking the tools and strategies to finally set you on the road to creating your unique and most respected brand, and as you use these tools and strategies, great results will start showing up in your business, career and life.

I have a secret to share with you. Although it should not come as a surprise to you. Most brands will fail at their goals. And the only thing that is more disheartening than all the failed brands out there is the cluelessness of many entrepreneurs and business executives about what branding REALLY is? Many assume that branding is simply designing a logo. However, the logo is just an aspect of the visual creation for the brand which also entails creating an effective positioning, values, website, tag line, ad copy, PR, sales and marketing campaign.

But branding does not stop at these elements. Less tangible aspects such as how the executive team and employees conduct themselves, as well as the general corporate culture, all form part of the DNA of the brand. As you understand all this, you will be on your way to making your brand the success you have envisioned. Therefore read on to find out how to create your outstanding brand?.

Let's get started!

Principles shared here may seem to be most aligned to organizations however these are the similar fundamentals you need to develop your personal brand. So please study them carefully.

My Apple is Branded

What is a Brand?

- Your Brand is your Unique Perceived Identity.

It is Unique- because it is uncopyable and unmatchable.

It is Perceived- because it is how you are known as by your market place and market is doing this consciously or subconsciously. This perception is in customers' mind.

It is Identity- because it states who you are.

E.g. Think about Google, Nike, Coca Cola, and Apple. Each one of them have Unique Perceived Identity and that is their brand.

My Apple is Branded

Now you may ask, **What is Branding?**

- Branding is a Conscious and Consistent process of Brand Building i.e. Creating desirable associations in customers' mind.

It is a Conscious process because it must be well-planned, deliberate and strategic process.

It is a Consistent process because it must be an ongoing process, which never and must not stop.

E.g. Once again think about Google, Nike, Coca-Cola, and Apple. Each one of them is making deliberate efforts to stay visible to you.

You have certain known or unknown expectations from these brands and they are full-filling it, making you trust them or grow your trust on them about their identity.

You get certain feelings when you trust someone and you get the exact same feelings when you trust these brand's identities. And this is their competitive advantage- Making them unique and different from their competition.

Customers enjoy buying the products and services of these brands.

When you are a brand, customers do not pay for just products or services- they are really paying for raising their own value. They feel pride by owning products of these brands. E.g. Customers feel pride in buying Nike Shoes or Apple iPhone etc.

(A)

SECRETS behind Successful Brands

My Apple is Branded

Whether it was launched just an year ago or has been around for the last century, some businesses just seem to have the Midas touch when it comes to attracting attention and establishing themselves as favorites amongst their customers.

Certainly, this Midas touch does not happen all by itself. Successful brands have figured out how to work their way into the hearts, minds and wallets of their customers. It might be because of their compassionate ways to convey the brand message, sense of community or sensible pricing.

During my research I've discovered some common features in all the brands. Here are they. Their top secrets.

Secret #1:

Every brand has Unique Identity in at least one area:

Google leads the internet search engine area, Nike is in sportswear, Coca-Cola is in carbonated soft drinks where as Apple is in consumer electronics.

All of these massive brands have at least one area where they have established expertise and that way their Unique Identity.

Secret #2:

Every brand is consistently visible:

> When is the last time you had heard or seen something about Google, Nike, Coca-Cola or Apple? I can assure you that not too long ago. All the big brands make consistent efforts to stay visible to their customers. Because they know "Out of Sight means Out of Mind".

Secret #3:

Every brand delivers its brand promise:

> Successful brands focus on delivering their brand promise by designing products which their customers wants to own (not just need or buy…but Own).
> They do this by broadcasting what they will do and they fulfill that promise.
>
> Xerox is the ultimate example. It has delivered its brand promise so great that we now substitute the word 'copy' by 'Xerox'.

Secret #4:

Every brand creates an Ultimate user experience:

> When customers own products or services from branded companies they get the feeling that their own value has gone up. And that is the ultimate user experience. These brands make the users feel more significant compared to the users who own the competition products.
>
> They create an experience that will have their customers talking to their friends for a long time. Ask any successful brand and they will tell you that word-of-mouth advertising accounts for a huge chunk of their sales and traffic.
>
> Ask any iPhone owner and he will show you his pride and feeling of significance over competitors' mobile phone users.

Secret #5:

Every brand has demonstrated the results:

> Every successful brand has strong backing of world-class results they have produced in the past. E.g. Apple has Mac, iPhone series, iPod etc.
>
> Customers now trust them because these brands have demonstrated proven results.
> Take another example of cricket legend Sachin Tendulkar. He has become a sports star because he has demonstrated the results in his area of expertise.

Secret #6:

Every brand is more than just its products or services:

> Successful brands attract a loyal following of customers / consumers who feel connected to it and what it stands for.

> Shoppers think of the brand as a community and that by purchasing the brand, they are in fact buying into something bigger.

> Therefore the brand is just not about the products or services. It is bigger than that. It is the big perceived value by the customers / consumers.
> e.g. Think about this: How do you feel if you are driving a Ferrari Vs any ordinary car. Both are means of transport however perceived value of what you are buying is very different.

Secret #7:

Every brand is an intelligent marketer:

Learn to market with people and not at them.

Successful brands are built on buzz. They are there everywhere their target audience hangout.

They consistently promote products or services that leaves their customers feeling great about themselves and the products / services they buy.

E.g. Coca-cola or Pepsi. Watch any world-class sports events. You will see their banners, posters and commercials about them. And if you have not noticed before, see which soft drink's name is in your mind when you go shopping for it.
It's not due to the products, its due to brand's promotion.

Secret #8:

Every brand not just quickly adapts, but leads the changes in the market place:

> All the successful brands are in constant touch with their customers and they make every attempt to understand their customers' current and future needs. Therefore as the customer is stepping into future they have the products ready to serve them. E.g. Apple introduced series of products under iPod and iPhone brand. Microsoft did the same for its Microsoft windows, MS office packages.

Secret #9:

Every brand has built family of products and services:

Once you trust the brand, you don't mind buying from it often and also buying different products or services from that brand.

Therefore Big brands tend to have a family of products and services. And without us noticing, they share a big chunk of activities in our life. E.g. Google has search engine, but it also has Gmail, You tube, Drive, Chrome, Play, Maps etc. If you are a Nike fan see what else you have bought from Nike along with the foot wear.

Secret #10:

Every brand in itself is a promise:

> Every brand makes certain unique promise based on the values it will stand for. In many cases, you can check the tagline to get the values these brands stand for.
>
> Values form the core skeleton of the brand and every activity is then evolved out of value.
>
> E.g. BMW. Its tag line is 'The ultimate driving machine'
>
> For Apple, it is 'Think different'
>
> BMW and Apple products deliver their promises.

Secret #11:

Every brand has certain key elements which helps them distinguish from their competition to make it easily recognizable to its customers.

a) Logo: The visual identity of the brand.
b) Name: The word or words used to identify a company, product, service, or concept.
c) Tagline: It is the catch phrase.
d) Colours: Think about Facebook, Skype's logos. They have their unique colours.
e) Some brands also have other elements such as Sounds, Scents, Movements, Tastes, Customer experience.

Secret #12:

It takes time to establish the brand:

It takes time to deliver consistent results. It takes time to get the clarity to customers about who you are, what you do and what you stand for. It takes time to generate fans. It takes time to establish the brand. It is never an overnight success.

My Apple is Branded

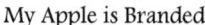

Don't just build a business, build a Brand. A Rich
and Successful Brand!

~ Success Coach Nilesh

My Apple is Branded

B)

PROCESS of Creating Your Outstanding Brand

The brand is not just a logo. It is a promise that your customers can believe in. The promise of who you are and the value you deliver, that will be reinforced with every single interaction customers has with any part of your organization. A successful brand will build name awareness, make selling easier, create customer loyalty, and increase the odds of survival for your business. But most importantly, a successful brand will always make you money.

To make your job easy, here is the process of creating your outstanding brand.

1) Decide your "WHY?":

This is the million dollar question (or may be a billion dollar if you are aiming high). Understanding or defining the WHY behind your need for Brand creation will give you the required logical and emotional pull (and push) to establish your brand.

E.g. When Narayana Murthy of India set up Infosys, in one of his interviews he had mentioned that his goal was to create the most respected IT company. That became his WHY in creating Infosys as a respected brand name in the IT industry.

Your WHY helps you and directs you in every strategic decision making process. Therefore first decide your WHY.

2) Decide Your "WHO?":

At this moment I want to share the famous quote from Arnold Schwarzenegger. He had said:

"Dig deep down inside you and ask yourself WHO do you want to become, not WHAT but WHO".

As you know Arnold Schwarzenegger as the greatest body builder and his quest for WHO helped him work hard, take the precise decisions, and acquire the desired focus to become successful and rich in his life.

In the similar manner, ask yourself WHO do you want to become, in your eyes and in the eyes of your customers? What feeling do you want to give them? What else can you do for them? Can you save time for them? Can you save money for them? Add value or give them respect? Or Do you want to become bigger, better, faster or easier than the existing brands etc. There is a technical term for this process and it is called as Brand Positioning.

Brand Positioning is the term given to the process of consciously locating a market niche (a distinctive place) to build your brand into the minds of customers. This involves differentiating your offering, and thereafter inserting it into a free space in the market to fulfill a need that has remained unfulfilled. This will require targeted marketing and communications strategy. Your branding strategy serves as the big-picture insight that will guide your marketing activities to ensure that they lead to success.

In other words, Brand Positioning is the way by which the brands create a distinct impression in the customer's mind.

Effective Brand Positioning depends upon identifying and communicating the brand's uniqueness, differentiation and verifiable value. It is important to note that 'me too' brand positioning contradicts the notion of differentiation and should be avoided at all costs. This type of copycat brand positioning only works if the business offers its solutions at a significant discount over the competitor(s).

3) Trust Yourself:

Believe that you can reach the position where you want to reach. Then lay out the steps to get there. Many people and leaders in the organizations never believe that they can become bigger and better. Therefore they ignore to take any steps towards it and they stay mediocre. That is reason many small businesses stay small. If you have small business it doesn't mean you should think small. Think Big and Believe you will get there by following the required strategies.

As Zig Ziglar has said, "You don't have to be great to start but you have to start to become great"

4) Align your internal resources to start your journey towards becoming an outstanding Brand:

It does not matter whether you are an individual, a small company, a medium company or a big organization. When you decide to become a brand, you first have to 'Become' what you have to be seen as.

E.g. If you want to be an Olympic gold medalist then you first have to become the athlete who can win the gold medal.

If you want to own a successful business then you first have to become the businessperson who can succeed.

This may sound like a very simple strategy, but if you fail to understand it, you will waste endless time, money, and energy in wondering or doing the things which can never make you an outstanding brand.

Communicate with your team, make them aware of where you want to reach as an organization, broadcast the unique message which is congruent with your ultimate brand goal. Become 'One Team' serving 'One Goal'.

5) Take Steps to Create the Right Impression:

What should /would / must people think about you, talk about you and share about you; when you are in front of them or even when you are not in front of them? Every day the average customer encounters hundreds of promotional messages. This forces them to only tune in to messages that are unique, consistent, different, attractive, and which appeal to their needs and wants. To grab the attention of customers and keep their custom, you need a brand promise that matches their desire and expectations. Create a unique, simple and strong face and voice for your brand, one which truly represents your business. This should be consistent in tone and image across all your marketing communications.

➢ Invest Time (& money if needed) in designing Your Logo / Company name / Tag line – The logo is the most important expression of a brand. Get a professionally designed logo and compliment it with a tagline that sums up your offering. Make a tag line which customers can relate, use and remember it. Make sure your company name is in sync with the brand you are planning to create. Make sure you are using the influential colours.
E.g. Yellow = Optimism, Green = Wealth, Blue = Trust and Sincerity, Red = Energy and Urgency, Orange = Aggressive, Pink = Romantic, Black = Powerful, and Purple = Soothing and Calming

Make the company name Easy, Catchy, Unique, Different and Valuable from **customers' point of view**. Many times what makes sense to you may not make sense to customers.

➢ Secure Your Intellectual Property (IP): It is extremely important to protect your hard work and identity. Therefore I highly advise to protect your logo, tag line and company name. Just do a google search to get the IP registration process of your country.

➢ Create a Theme – Create a consistent theme for all your marketing materials so as to express your brand personality and make it memorable.

➢ Be Consistent – Repetition builds reputation. Ensure that every single element of your brand is correctly and consistently presented to your market. Customers must see your advertising many times, consistently, may be via multiple media channels. However you must also focus on word of mouth promotions

➢ Deliver Your Promise – Brand does not exist if there are no results to back it. Consistently create the results promised by your brand and present the verbal and visual elements of your brand to your market. It will also attract new customers. You just have to keep delivering your promise to retain and grow their community.

6) Promote your brand:

Be it the launch of a new brand or revitalizing an existing one, you will need to promote your brand identity as part of a complete brand story. When preparing for your brand launch:

➢ Launch a PR program that will get your brand message into the market
➢ Promote your brand to your target market
➢ Plan your launch event to the finest detail. Decide what results you want and make relevant plans.
➢ Promote via multiple media channels e.g. Newspapers, online, social media, your network etc.
➢ Encourage feedback
➢ Follow up enquiries or sales leads

7) Keep Your Brand Fresh and Relevant

It is vital to keep the presentation of your brand looking fresh and relevant over the years in order to keep up with the changing markets and cultural reference points.

➢ Regularly review your marketing materials
➢ Remain updated with changing market trends
➢ Regularly communicate with customers

Brands just don't sell products or services, they build relationships.

~   Success Coach Nilesh

My Apple is Branded

(C)

Where should you START?

My Apple is Branded

To make your Brand building process easier for you, I am going to share with you a very simple analogy.

Building a brand is like building a house. Both endeavors require a location. As your house needs a plot, the brand requires a position in the market place. Both also need a plan to follow so as to achieve the outcome you desire. Both of them require investment of time, money and resources. Both of them need protection. If you nurture them carefully their value will go up.

Following are the unique steps designed to help you position, plan and create your rich and successful brand that will help you achieve the goals of your business.

Step #1: Decide what you want to Brand.

First decide whether you will be branding your company or a product or service. It is advisable to create one strong brand for your business, and thereafter extend that brand to cover everything that your business has to offer. This will increase brand equity and create a circle of recognition. The alternative would be to build a business full of brands which could be expensive, time-consuming and confusing to your customers. However, if this is your best solution, ensure that you create a stand-alone profit center for every new brand so that you will be able to track its performance.

Step #2: Decide why you want to Brand.

Once you have decided what you have to brand (Company, Product or Service), find out the reasons why. Make a list of reasons why you have finalized that decision. This list will help you in all the strategic decisions that you will make in the future.

Step #3: Do Your Homework.

The key to building a successful brand is research and lots of it. Understand your customers: who they are, what they want and where they are, what do they really need and care about? Once you grasp their needs, wants and desires, this will provide you with a sound foundation to build your brand and grow your entire organization around it, supporting it.

Ask the following questions before you decide to position your brand.

- Who are your real target customers?
- How many are they?
- Where they live?
- What lifestyle do they lead?
- How much is their monthly earning power?
- Why should they buy from you?
- How much would they be willing to pay?
- Have they previously heard of your product or company? If so, where from?
- Where would they typically go to source this type of product or service?
- Have they previously sourced it elsewhere? If so, where and why?
- What websites do they visit?
- What magazines/ newspapers/ TV channels/ shows/ radio stations do they subscribe to?
- What logical reasons you will need to promote to your customers?
- Which emotional triggers you will need, to influence their buying decisions?

Step #4: Define Your Offering.

Once you are in full grasp of the wants, needs, desires and expectations of your customers, revisit your offering and begin to lay the foundation for a brand that will accurately reflect the essence of what your business will stand for, who you will serve, what you will promise and how you will operate.

➢ Decide your Brand Position- The place where you want to be seen by your customers.
  Ask yourself WHO do you want to become, in your eyes and in the eyes of your customers. What feeling do you want to give them? What else can you do for them? Can you save time for them? Can you save money for them? Add value or give them respect? Or Do you want to become bigger, better, faster or easier than the existing brands etc. How you want to differ from your competitors? (Current competitors and future 'would be' competitors).

  You can also use the **future look back** strategy.
  Imagine and think about the future of your brand somewhere after 1-3 years. See where you want to reach? What do you want your customers to tell others about you? What should media, newspapers, TV should say about you?
  Write down all this and then decide the road map to reach there from the present condition. Trust yourself that you will get there by implementing certain strategies.

➢ Identify Your Values – Values are the set of principles which guide you how to operate in the market place. To decide your values find out the following:
  ▪ What you are and what you are not willing to do to achieve success?
  ▪ What are the fundamentals your business will stand for?

- Which key words you want your customers to associate with you?
- What do you assure customers who come into contact with your business?
- What expectations you'll live up to each time customers experience your brand?
- A friendly warning: Avoid making promises that you cannot consistently deliver on.

In summary, from all of the answers above, decide to be well known for **one big thing** (That will be your uniqueness, your expertise)

Step #5: Create your brand identity. Invent or confirm your brand name. Design your logo and tag line. You will need to ensure that it is the true reflection of the attributes of your brand. Please see the appendix as a guide for choosing your logo, company name and tag line. Please take professional help where needed.

Step #6: Protect your brand identity. I would highly recommend you to protect your hard work by registering the intellectual property. (Trademark / Copyright / Patent)

Step #7: Become the identity which you will be promoting. Become the expert you want to be seen as.

Step #8: Start the promotion and marketing activities.

Step #9: Keep creating consistent and relevant results which will reinforce the promises you are making through your brand. In Brand Building process, it is not just first but 2nd , 3rd...all impressions matter.

Step #10: Stay visible to your customers. As you are consistently visible with unique message; customers will start to notice you. They will like you, they will trust you and they will buy from you.

Step #11: Create, maintain and grow your fans and their community. Communicate with them. Stay in touch. Grow your network. Many companies use news letters or periodic press releases to keep in touch with the customers.

Step #12: Adapt, change and keep leading the market place in your area of specialization. Be that identity which your customers are willing to attach them and feel proud to talk about them

Branding is an ongoing process. You will need to repeat the steps 7 to 12. Every successful brand does and you should do it too. You will reap massive rewards if you follow these.

This is one of the most exciting things you do when you start your own company. A winning company name is the one which you will use to pull business in itself.

Here are my top tips on how to choose your company name:

1. **Do not limit yourself:** Try to avoid choosing a name that is sector limiting as this would put you in trouble if in future you decide to expand your business. E.g. SeaFoods Pvt. Limited will be a good name for a seafood related business however it will limit your brand to extend in other industries.

   Before confirming the name make sure you visit the internet to check if that word does not mean something far different, that you originally intended, when translated to some other language. If it does, then again you would be in trouble if you later decide to expand your business overseas.

   General Motors launched their Nova car in Spain however later they found that Nova in Spanish means 'it does not go'. Therefore research your brand name for meanings in different cultures and countries.

2. **Be inspired:** Look around for inspiration and get creative. If possible hold a brainstorming session with your friends, family members and team.

3. **Convey the right impression:** Make sure that you convey the right message and impression about your company to your potential customers. E.g. Häagen-Dazs is an Ice cream brand in Europe and USA however in many parts

of India Häagen is linked with an awkward thing. So stay careful with foreign names.

4. **Know the laws:** Make sure you are aware of all the rules and regulations that are to be followed when deciding the name of your business. Make sure that you don't sound too much like an existing brand or business as this would only put you in trouble later.
   Every country has specific rules about naming the company. Do an online research to find out rules for your country.

5. **Consider spelling and pronunciation:** Your company name should not be something that can be easily misspelled. Also it is you who would suffer if your company name is not easy to pronounce for everyone as you would need to give out the details of your company, a lot of times through media. E.g. Eggcetera is tough to remember for the unfamiliar people.

6. **Keep it short and simple:** Once again, this is important as people should be able to tell about it to others and also for the promotional purposes. Also a long name will not do you any good. It should be short and simple! E.g. Apple, Skype etc.

7. **Be careful about acronyms:** Choose the acronyms, if they can form some simple or easy to remember names. If it can be meaningful then it is even great. E.g. DIY shops in UK stands for Do It Yourself. It sells the tools and parts which need minimal professional help to assemble or install.

8. **Check Availability:** Do your research and check if the name is already being used. Research to find if anyone else has got a registered trademark under this name.

9. **Get feedback:** Try to get feedback from as many people as you can before you formally commit to that name.

But finally, make sure that YOU really like your company name because you might see yourself waking up with this name, every single day.

Tips for Logo Design

Logo design is not simple. It is not just writing the name of your company in a circle. Only a well thought and designed logo will be successful. A logo is your company's first impression and can impact a customers' attitude towards your products and services.

To get you started, I would like to share with you few tips that can help you design a successful logo which can give your company that great first impression.

1. **Know your audience:** Understand the target market before you start designing the logo. Know which audience the brand is for, so that you can consider the other elements for the logo. For example, a childish font and colour scheme will be appropriate for a toy shop but not for an accountancy firm!

2. **Give importance to color:** Even colours have meanings. They communicate ideas. It may still work in greyscale but colour(s) bring life to the logo.

3. **Do not be tempted to imitate:** Be inspired but try not to imitate someone else's logo..

4. **Use negative spaces effectively, if you can:** Try to make some hidden meanings in the negative space. For example, if you look up the logo of 'FedEx', you will see that they have used the space between E and x to create an arrow.

5. **Understand cultural differences:** Usually motion towards left means going backwards while motion towards right means moving forward and positive. This developed mainly because we read from left to right. There are places in the world where they read from right to left. So understand this difference while designing your logo.

6. **Check for hidden words:** If you are styling your logo such that all the letters are in the same case, then be careful that it does not spell any unintended word in between. For

example, some people noticed a rude word when the 'weightwatchers' logo decided to go all small case.

7. **Be simple:** Do not include too many things in your logo. It does not need to show the entire history of your company. If it is made simple and unique, then it can be easily memorised and recognised by your customers.

8. **Be meaningful**: Instead of making a logo by just drawing some lines or curves, make something which has an inner meaning to it. For example, if we take the logo of 'Toyota', it is not just a fancy 'T'. The central overlapping ovals represent faith and trust between the company and its customers, whereas the encircling outer oval represents their global expansion plans.

A great logo will become your visual identity for your customers. Therefore use the logo which conveys the message that you really want to convey. No need to complicate it. Keep it simple.

Tips for Company Tag line Design

Creating a successful tag line is what most people fail at. It definitely is not an easy task. Tag line should be simple but exciting and memorable. There is absolutely no need to overcomplicate it.

Here are some tips to help you deign your successful Tag line:

1. **Know your target market:** Understand your company's business interests and work on your tag line according to that. For example, if your company is targeting older people, then use words that they would like.

2. **Should be positive:** Research has found that negative statements do not sell well. So go for positive statements. E.g. Stillwell Ford had a Tag line: We put people in front of cars. I think you got the meaning.

3. **Focus:** The tag line should not be very long. A few words itself should make it standout. Do not try to say a lot in your tag line. Keep it simple so that your vision can be easily understood by your potential customers as well as your employees.

4. **Should be in context:** Your name, logo and tag line should go in harmony with each other. The colour, font and size should complement each other. There should be correct balance among these for your logo to be successful.

5. **Brainstorm:** Write on a sheet of paper whatever words that come to your mind about your company. Writing it down like this is better than thinking it in your mind. Get help from your trusted friends and family members.

6. **Make it memorable:** Be creative. If you want, try to bring an interesting twist to a normal phrase or a positive subtle double meaning. If there is something like this in your tag line, then people will talk about it and thus they themselves will end up doing some marketing for you!

7. **Be honest:** You can easily get carried away while thinking of a tag line. Be honest about your company and what you actually provide.

8. **Keep it consistent:** Once you formally declare your tag line to public, stick to it. Do not keep changing it often because you think it has become boring. Upgrade if needed however avoid frequent changes after launch.

9. **Make sure it is readable:** Do not make the font size too small such that it becomes difficult to read. Also choose your font style wisely.

10. **Ask for feedback:** Get some of your trusted peers to review your tag line honestly. But do not keep rewriting because they ask you to. Just get their suggestions and ask yourself if you like it or not.

In short, great tag lines do not just happen. You have to spend a great deal of thought and time into it. But it will not be in vain as this is one important element that will draw attention from your potential customers.

Conclusion:

Creating an outstanding brand will be easy if you follow steps mentioned in this book. As you decide your brand positioning, the promise you want to deliver to your customers and include these in your marketing; you will find you are broadcasting focused message. Your customers will notice you. They will start to differentiate your uniqueness among your competitors. By offering a memorable user experience to your customers, you will begin your journey to create a successful brand. But do not stop there. Work at keeping your brand fresh and relevant for the years to come.

Remember that while talent can help get your business up and running, it is your brand that will lead it in the long term.

All the Best. Now go and create your outstanding brand. You have the potential. You can do it.

What you read SHAPES what you think and what you think SHAPES what you achieve in your life.

Thank you for choosing this book. This will transform your life.

~ Success Coach Nilesh

Other books from Success Coach Nilesh:

Go For Success

Best Selling Book of Success Strategies

Proudly Marketed and Sold by

Major online book retailers & www.SuccessCoachNilesh.com

Grab your copy

Read it – Gift it – Recommend it

www.ingramcontent.com/pod-product-compliance
Lightning Source LLC
Chambersburg PA
CBHW071807170526
45167CB00003B/1206